Don't Let Them See Me Like This

JASMINE GIBSON

Nightboat Books
New York

ISBN: 978-1-937658-83-0

Cover design by HR Hegnauer
Design and typesetting by Margaret Tedesco
Text set in Carta Magna, Neon Block, and Adobe Garamond Pro
Cover and title page photograph (detail) by John Rufo

Cataloging-in-publication data is available from the Library of Congress

Nightboat Books
New York
www.nightboat.org

Dedicated to the named and those who live, love and die without names.

TABLE OF CONTENTS

BENDER

We use surveillance for us
como se dice
cynicism is exactly what we need
and even what the F.A.I. (at some point)
had a willingness to die for
the opposite, non-mirror of a futurist manifesto
drawing blood in speeding motor cars
twisting viscous
holding courage, sensuality and fear
in both hands and feeling it slip through
continuing to snap until
we damn near break off from our own trunks
we know the state is collecting our image
for a time when we'll remember, maybe incorrectly
"we were 'more' free then, right?"

what are we going to do when politicians and superstars
aren't problematic anymore?

will you let the enemy in
when they say they appreciate the way yr ancestors died
to give you that pretty brown skin that glows
under the floodlights or
how nameless dead bodies are now the ultimate aesthetic
accepting the bourgeois death drive
and how radical is it when our desire
for freedom gets recuperated in the shape of an ugly boxy silk dress

all the women and not women, I know
are returning to points of youth
to regain something they lost
whether that's the thickness of their eyebrows
or feeling safe enough to love with abandon
and hurt there
it's too risky in this older body
too many holes, and not enough suitors filling the holes
with anything special or nourishing
just making the holes wider and more brittle
watch me break all over you

it's exhausting just finding a place to rest
to clean wounds like this

yes, I've been up deep into the night
when it's day where you are
thinking of ways to get out from underneath your skin
and no one is home

please burn my collection of poems
because now I know
that your love and ferocity were spent on another

in an American South

we can have it good
and it can be delicious
we can be dangerous like that

living without redemption
a hungry ghost, wandering, seeking its head
which is something much more

damn, you want my marrow too?

I thought you were a vampire
but you're excavating deeper
into the history in my blood and mess rooms

it's holy work, and I find pilgrims everywhere I go

I stared into the abyss and knew I loved her then
because only she could appreciate how I fall apart
sopping wet and still manageable even if I'm wrong
and that's good enough
knowing you could never afford my love

STOP TEXTING ME

Thousands of militants in the streets

Want to cum in ecstasy

More than the government's will to strangle them

Thousands of prisoners want to be free

And to taste air on skin

In the remnants of the carceral state

Burning, still smoking at dawn

When we're all free

In defense of demons

We build your walls

So that you can be the last white man

To die within it

THE FOOL

A future in a different city that can't be seen because there's a sea between
maybe if there was no capitalism, then I could truly love you the way we both deserve
maybe if there was no schedule, time tables or global warming, I'd be with you again
but there isn't and love matches airline miles and market demand
an invisible hand touching me in the shower, me moaning into your mouth
I finally found the diaspora
under a faucet in the new world

STOP TEXTING ME

Black like

How am I gonna enclose upon you

Like motherfucker tell me what's real

On a Tuesday, hold your skin close to mine

rub and tell me you've never

felt how the moon could move under you like that

How insurrection is just the thickening of lining

and we're either going to abort, bleed or give birth

Doesn't it get you wet?

HEAVY METAL

Who knew that organs could weigh so much and absorb a city's abuses
Katrina or Flint
repeated events can feel like fate
the question
"are you sure what you put in your body isn't killing you?"
or
"this is a personal issue"
but
whatever
new heavy metal is in season
whether it's liquid or alkaline like
it still cakes onto your liver and lungs like
that lover you want back but
you remember all of the disasters
that came along with the relationship

All my goddesses are heavy metal
because they were all burnt
on hot irons at sea, in small villages, backyards
with burning crosses and borders so segmented
they split the body in two
but can still breathe and take
in toxins and heavy metals
and don't that make you feel fucking expansive
like my god
your body on mine and how I want you to melt on my tongue
kinda heavy metal

This is your welcome party
This is your potluck

It is an orientation that you woke up late for
and ran 2 hours late to and realized you missed nothing at all
and the body sags at the wasted time of linens
on ashen skin that you have to go 3.5 hours to touch and
27 doors and 1600 flights of stairs
to be reunited once again and it still doesn't feel as good
as the lies you told yourself about
how good it would feel
These are calculations for how you have to strain to shit
Even the little that comes out matters

What about Syrians and legitimate pain
When you realize the government
class collaborators and landowners
heads of breeding
have always had a grip on yr uterus
you can feel it when it lurches and
not when "daddy" was a metaphor but
an actual apparatus of reproduction of stock
excavation as self critique
so that you may feel the depth
of your flesh
light wounds can be mortal too

Does your guilt keep others awake or is it just you?
trusting yourself to be honest with yourself
based on the fact that you are not
that different from what you are fighting?
when war makes a sound like that

how it keeps you up at night
how theory dies when it leaves your lips

All my expansiveness is heavy metal
and it's not my business what you think about me
there can be a conversation in code but it cannot
rid heavy metal from the soul

Am I being detained and what summoned your presence
We only mourn blacks who die
for peace treaties and reasons
that ultimately don't lead us to liberation
And don't let me tell you about the maroon blood
that scares away the Indio skin
that so many white lovers benefit from
"Yes, it's true. I can feel it when your
fingers are inside me and right there.
Yes, there, I'm cumming and present.
I woke up in the middle of it all."

There is a whole history of people lying about where they were born
and forgetting where they got married
because the seams unraveled too quickly
due to impacts missing in state records
county records but apparent in body records
Breeding
Like
"I came upon this shore in heavy metal"

Banks get wet at the idea of millions of bodies breaking
salivating over the fat, bloated profitable organs
It's expensive to be this poor

When the checks hit all at once don't look at the balance
Balance is false and mocking
Balance is the manipulation of striving and straining
Balance is the blood in your stool
You can't live like that
Looking down into the toilet bowl, and seeing maroon, saying
"Lord, give me the strength
and balance to make it through this day"

How many theorists does it take to essentialize the breakdown of the body
due to the working day
And was it a relief when purely genetics was to blame

HOT-HAND FALLACY

In the woods many things can happen
there are coyotes who sound like yelping children on hot leather seats in summer
I reach out for your abdomen
there are others watching
and truth be told, they knew before we knew before we met the sea
whether it be the blackness of my hair or the darkening of my skin under the sun
the ocean always knew
I could tell by how the salt water stayed in my sinuses and burned you there
it was cruel and full of shadow

You couldn't tell me the name of the place
instead of it being a place it was something larger
a street

A street lovers fought on, a street where
people throw projectiles at pigs
and that is truly romance, isn't it?
throwing a Molotov at the cops, watching
everything catch fire and believing in that moment we are free
a real release
but we go back to our jobs anyway the next day
stealing time, talking in bathrooms and saying
how much we learned and won't repeat and of course the
"I miss you but we can't speak like this"

I got a fat lip in the dark on that street
on the edge of a car door

It hit me so hard in the darkness
I thought I'd lose a tooth and future suitors
then I thought
I'll be so beautiful then, a larger gap to
fit more things in, things that can live rather than die there
the blood is a courtesy and proves
my tooth was alive at one point
that I had once given enough energy caring for that tooth
and the root that lays in it. It's soft, pink and still a child.
and I would have aborted that child, for the sake of new vanity
a missing tooth, beneath a palm tree
and a bleeding hole painting my lips
the same color as MAC's "Ruby Woo"

I felt all of my insides on that street
I felt how they moved around
made space for
and squeezed in response to life on that street
doing everything in the broadness of the dark
against the neighborhood of mutated life
suburban life that no one can afford

I am reading all of this backwards,
to understand you better
you bite
I bite back
I want you to eat me
I want to stick to the back of your throat

because I deserve to be that knot
that doesn't go away when you drink water
I want it
I want 'it'
because it is sticky sweet lies within the lines
not the part about confused offices or heroic leaps
of faith on bridges or barricades or
even the fucking mascot of us all
a goddam riot dog
but about how you slept and who that happened with
and how your skin felt as you did it
what it felt like to be weak and muted
and when you dreamt of plunges
swimming as you dreamed about brown moodiness
and how it coated the teeth

All the 30-year-old theory sad boys want to be you
they want to be gods and ache like you
they wanna know what the protests were like,
man
not about the women that held you up
protected you from tear gas
definitely not those who reproduced your ass to see another day

I don't think I've hated something so much as me wanting you
the impossibility of your depth
upon finite puddles
finite masses

running on pure lack and ashen molten flesh
and nothing could be as pure as your lazy tongue moving against me
I've asked you to go harder
and you could only go hard on guilt
betrayal
Broken windows are our only commons
and I've learned that the term "honky" emerged
from boys
like you can't hold
girls like me
instead
they can hold them in cars
do seats on different coasts always feel as indifferent?

Cut to scene
I am crying in the dark
this is not justified
you shrink because that's what ordinary men do
when they're doing all that they can
when a woman like that yelps in the dark
trysts over breakfast and blackening emptiness forming
these things can't happen when you're against 'things'

HENRIETTA LACKS

The lining is all gone

full of ulcers and bondage slavery

think of it as an inheritance

the kind that runs by blood

and air that will never reach your heart
or exit out of the cadaver's hands

that have now become a part of your
own extremities
I never said I didn't navel gaze, I just
said I forgot what pines smelt like
Pinus

The brain is swimming
in a pond on Pluto
the body is shutting down
you are not allowed to leave this potluck
the heart palpitates
while you wonder
how you'll have to fight with your co-workers
over who gets to take their lunch break first and
¿como tienes pelo malo?

Sugar makes me clot
and ache for a child
poetry is very much like schizophrenia
fixations on the fear of a hysterectomy
meant to rectify any inner forgiveness
the voices of guilt hug the lines
I am learning to be vulnerable

Look at Maluca go
watch as the working day eats into her limbs
making her hole
watch as the tips insufficiently fill it
has she ever felt so empty and less full
It's a deeper knowledge than knowing what hunger feels like

In a softness of my own

Drunk on possibility
Screaming my own name on the sidewalk on my back

Was the party as bad as I thought

SUOMI

All of this sprawl could be afforded by a few for the cost of the sea
a boring archipelago, with pretty lovers screaming Finnish in their sleep
they want to leave too
they know what's good
or at least how to make things right
I'm right here
and yes, we are both surprised by how we can love like this
it's surprising,
I mean, like you and me
and the photographs that haven't been taken
then there's the skin that may stretch and
carry, whether that belongs to me or you
I'm still trying to smell you on my skin
my body is cramping in my arms, trying to make myself small
especially when

Niggers,
in broad sense, but like me also
like
Somos Nosotros Negros
were never meant to reach northern wet cities
like Helsinki
you can tell by the narrow city streets and the blinding white churches
not meant to touch my flesh, but instead extract from ivory bones
yes, your family was amongst the poachers
with photographs smiling back
my great great grandmother making love and hate to a coolie on soggy banks
In rags

In wonderment, that in every language there is a disdain for blackness
in every phrase, there is a code for being wary of darkness
even on the filmy surfaces of pools
rattling in a metal ribcage, over dead rivers and ice melts
will it ever be warmer than this?
the mercury in the fish made me horny for you
and this was even after people on
the street avoided eye contact with me,
"...You know how hard it is for me to
Shake the disease"

Sleepover
to sleep away
it's the social democracy we died for
the social democracy
If I don't hold the gaze, my image gets distorted or worse
lost
I didn't have to break the sea in half
to know I'm not wanted here
the violence of domestication
is a history of grunts and spurting sounds
you can tell by the proximity of sounds and color
embedded in the lining
I am recording this to remember that
it is real

maybe I had a choice but that is of course up to the audience
Livsfarlig
I got so happy while writing this
I could barely finish
but then it all came back again
leaked onto me, you, and the bed sheets
"...I'm feeling much stranger about you..." :

You didn't need to threaten bondage on other lands
resources
property
gummy flesh
children
to not
not
benefit from whiteness
it's a blinding and unwavering light
it is rapture
there is no need for intimacy when your flesh is in proximity
it takes us all

How strong this is, even when it's broken against me
neither one of us belong here, in the North
America broke every highway into the woods
at first we descended from the sky, but then by boat
Dying to let you know,
brown does not equal "foreigner"
but can be a stranger in the village too

Brasil has always been a fiction
A place for escape
But not from property relations
Not even from nationalist projects
That crack bones wide open
And leave mothers to bleed right there
In what would become paved streets
We all know where samba comes from
And it isn't the city

We can all haunt white women until our heart's content
With or without 'place' in their names
Because there is no home or no land
And no shore to beach upon
If opportunity can be manifested
We can all be rich, make money
Have revenge melt all over our bodies
Because it feels good and it's immediate
Don't we all wanna cum through like that

When there isn't anything to risk

White people can speak any language

DRAPETOMANIA

Spanish is clumsy on my tongue like Angolan slaves
breaking their tools in Puerto Rico, Barbados and Nevis
Black women have killed their babies only
to save their souls from diabetes
and policemen coming to shoot them in their sleep
what do niggers dream while walking through a living nightmare?
the cost is some bargaining chip in a minor suburb of Michigan

My grand maimed one
and all the thick cocks of Missouri
that god could not hide from me

If I die, then let the city burn with me
I want my blackness to coat the cities' night
to burn like Sati's glowing skin
let the foundation shake
have the children eat from my flesh
to be reborn as heroes in Homer's Odyssey
if I am to die at the hands of our enemies, then use my corpse as a Golden Fleece
decapitate the cyclops in blue

Do you know what love feels like
to vibrate and violently shake
to watch *The Exorcist* late at night with the second love of your life
just to hear he became an uncle to a new life the next day
to feel wet in the middle of the night
like a moist tampon on the first day of a period
to truly be content

I go into the sea at night and let the waters lap at my charcoal-flavored labia
why are verdicts announced at night
"Are they scared?"
they should be
the whiskey bottle is mocking me with its Aunt Jemima form
I don't want to return
I don't know how to exchange fares at this destination
I will lose myself in the crisis
I don't want to return to work
I don't want to sleep and count the weeks
dedicated to
how much money I have to save for rent
I don't want to grovel paycheck to paycheck
I don't want to mutter under my breath when pigs show up to my workplace
I want to burn
I want everyone to know how alcohol feels when it's lit
what it's like to play with fire
I want us to burn today and tomorrow

LESSONS IN STARVATION

Your mother will compliment your figure
as psychosis pokes through the hips
"A historical materialist analysis of generational starvation: a comedy"
walk over to the lamppost and call out his name
Paris streets stink of barbecue and empty roosts
Brown bodies learn to float in all bodies of water
on coasts of the new and old world
it's called modernity
and the end of everything post-post

Do people really believe they have better things to do than struggle?
lovers whisper about imperialism, if you want them to
you can scream in the light, if you need to
we lie about our youth, just feel out flashbacks and trauma
god is blessing all those that feel negritude the most
doing the most
Inshallah

To die totally alone in our rooms
As the rub of subway doors hits along the seam of our jacket
Threatening "to open up"
Let it
Sniff into the glass and smell the poison
Drink deep
Condos and psych hospitals side by side so that you may find your way
Baby boy's mind shattered in the brothels of Puebla
Border Indian casinos for white anxieties

What did we find in that desert of memory

washed and paved in green on my soul

your soul

it's all the same but then again

it's not because white men's souls need saving

in these times

white men that did not die crossing westward

meeting a water demon, killing children and people that weren't children

could never be children because that's a "white thing"

a white stage, not granted to Caliban and folk

you must have found God, amongst the corpses

the dead livestock and the salty ocean

(NOW THEY WANT TO LAY PIPELINES, AND HAVE THE DOGS DO IT)

thanatos

not really interested in living tributes

but then again that's how well you found this casino

on a border of history, loaded heavy with guilt

anxiety because Reich said so

that casino, that dead,

fixed capital

casino

dead of deserted desire

not quite rotting

but dead all the same

I can taste it on the dollar bills stuffed into a fetish

On the phone with a lover, telling me their mother could get deported

back to a graveyard created and imported by the U.S.

the graveyard is U.S.D.A approved so

we can all be fed and bloated

it's not cannibalism, if it's organic and reused

and that's what the graveyard

I mean

casino is like

not damp, but plastic and glowing

with our deepest desires and use value waiting to be accumulated

SCHATZEN

Is this place old or was it built this way
flying through some unknown desert
in steel cages
imagining what lies beneath the hard plastic lining
it's fear
bouncing and rattling against unknown modules and
cheap plywood where the sound of debt creeps in
we all know that drought is coming
water got bored with immortality

I dreamt of you last night
cleaning up a scene no one would know about
carefully gathering clothes from the floor
without dropping a used condom in front of your wife
children
these are manic dreams
they no longer have meaning
I looked for an address but
there was a new development
plaster and silicon
a holy brickless vessel
can't you feel the divinity?
as if emotion has never touched your soul in this way before

I'm sure there is a German word for it

Pigeons live without names
but so do primary partners which is another way
to describe basic things like colors

Summer necrosis on polyester car seats
fall in upstate New York

I tried to cry and nothing came out
I cried when I came instead
it's nothing but cum
whilst the lord is by your side
and I can't because it doesn't work that way
I've tried to find you in the reflection of a puddle
In the ripped cartridges of yellow American spirits
In the pickling of my liver
None of those things were your style

In a bed of blood, hate and
desperation we found love in a state of insecurity
I've counted weeks and days and lost years dating back to: 24
or the coloring dye #23

Facsimile walls can't hold these wails
your hand couldn't find mine in the twilight of aging youth
we all ache for the desert at some point, don't we?
only to be laughed at by two or three gods out in these streets
we all want to open our veins and dry slowly sooner or later, *Claro*?
of course. Of course, you know what I've done
and how my hands tighten around your neck
gift wrapping paper on fire and bloated bellies over dim sum

OCEAN

As dust catches us

>Water clings to us, making everything coagulate together

>Death calls the border running along drenched spines of

>passageways

>It's the liquor that fills our brains

>As long as there is a drop of blood left in the body

>There can be a state of matter

>It's capital that sputters in our gestational tracts

>Alerting us to spells unknown, unseen ghosts in the dark

>The devil card, and ultimately, a new aborted world

>In the shape of a dying cow belly

>Feeding us nothing that we could not find

>This is abandonment in the purest form

>This is the coldness of indifferent serenity

>This is our comradeship at the end of inaugurations

>And the passing of garlands

>A queen appears

>"You have nothing. Turn your back to the cold"

>At her feet is scrawled

History happens upon the flesh, sitting

>Waiting to be introduced to mob theory

>Whether it's our world

>Versus

The barking of indolent dogs
Begging for the world to end in the shape of their image

Not waiting for fascism to die
Instead holding my mouth open
And crushing the state under my mandibles
Letting acidic fists do the rest
Collecting each flag until they become as adorned
As the bodies that continue to die for democracy

Only in the dark could I scream that something was wrong
Because my friends lit a flag on fire
That hung my body with rope
We cut that rope
From the intestines of the hierophant
The father, the family, the state,
The money and the cop
Then got born

I can feel it coming on like an echo

People have been dying on the cellular level
Alone in police jails

My body reminds you nothing of home
My body reminds you that everywhere is home
What you register as anger being legitimate is the constant state of pain
Like a wounded hellhound
Not crooning for the moon
But at the heaviness of history

The written word still holds weight
Wait
Like you say
In legal documents, like
Wait
You say
Eviction notices, how you say, court papers, wait
Jail documents, contract

Things of this
Nature
The weight of the written word has always been contractually binding
For things of this nature
Not dark not light, just misshapen and low
A dull screeching noise
And "how you say"
It on paper
The language of all free men
The weight, weighing down on others' ankles
Iron or plastic monitors
Wait, it doesn't matter

VERDE, TE QUIERO VERDE

There are definite tasks
Behind all that earth, behind all that cement
that lines prison and school yards
Where does God lie
When I cannot touch you?

I could count on a hand the months and years
that it takes to amount to Hegel's infinity
It is an equation with no answer and no future
Is it supposed to feel like this?
Am I supposed to be like this?
Queen of aches

I won't be here forever, especially once I delete this account
Why call it social media? Can't you call it what it is:
Wasteland, and other blank spaces like
"That really hurt _____. I didn't want it that way
But you made me. _____, you already knew about me, baby"
And who knew God could sneak into those tiny spaces

I tried to find you in the picture of hanging flowers
Feeling hard up, frustration sticking you in the side like Brutus' dagger
But I was Julius crying for you to come back or at least take me with you

I keep telling you it's not your fault, it's not my fault
It's no one's fault
And it's all our blame
And the historical process of
Marcus Garvey Park jutting into me like a monolith

STOP TEXTING ME

You really think you're free when there's ghosts

like Kalief Browder that haunt you?

He will be avenged

Coming in signs of three

1. A burning limo

2. The void

3. The crushing of white marble and the release

of a howl from the deepest part of the belly:

the disembowelment of slaveholders, in every definition of the title.

How the dead rose from their graves
Just to have their faces torn apart

The moon waits to be whole again

The sea broke in my face

I'll have to get old before anything else happens

We should all wonder about our grandparents' missing limbs

Violence against Women
As a form of checks and
Balances for
The margins of
Gender

Pain
Is a gendered history
Of lunatics
And bubonic Angels
Warning us of fire

This open sore
        I live in

                Where it is
        Considered
                Good fortune
                        Not to have been raped
                                        Capital has made every season
Cancer season

Seeing the sun set on birthed coasts
We laugh at Westerners searching for their souls and cultish gods
Ghosts scorched out in the open
By a dying sun

Uterus aching in the off-season
Skin facing sky

        And I'm a spirit on a timeline, not yet born. Things are just so evil
And that's the truth

SPINOZA'S LADDER

Foucault would call our "natural" inclination to submission,
"Governmentality",
While your bougie well-meaning friends reduce the farce,
That is our relationship to the biological anatomy of a swan.
We have no history, and there is no material to grip.

Trauma hunted me in the Bronx.
While you fucked fully clothed in Veracruz.
Now the state of trauma or State trauma has returned
To Welcome the anniversary of a dying marriage,
Children being born and other things discussed over eating barbecue.

We are others, naturally secretive.
You held my hand and I believed
That you were open when
What I saw was a crawl space. A gaslight. Is it true?
That mercury has been in retrograde for a year.
That my sullied sheets are our only home. Is it true?
What love can do and the violence it causes.

The state of violence. Or State violence.
Cats can only sleep when the police are at the door.
We've had two hours of sleep and you're surrendering
To rooms of potted plants
and stolen pictures of you and your wife in Quito.
You remind me that I am wrong about race.
I am reminded that there is only enough space for one forlorn woman.

Que Viva!

I am melting! And waking to phone calls from jail.

I cannot hear you

but the State is asking the expiration date on my debit card.

I did not tell you my vagina hurt when

I felt you place your fear in and out of me.

I remained wet. I confused passion for anxiety.

The latex dried and then you wept for the past ten years of your life.

OXBLOOD

Do you want my youth wrapped around your cock?
Love is fickle and forces one into the balminess of memory
Just to remember it's a false memory you're looking for
I got so busy looking at the past
I forgot to look up at the changing leaves

The people want their anthems and
Their black women, like their horses
Beat
Feeling no pain

Devil makes three:

Can you let black and brown people be righteous
When they're alive or will you continue leaving artificial flowers at electronic wakes?

It doesn't matter what "it" is or whether "it" could let "us" be
But rather "it" was
Communism as a place we could get to
And the love we could never realize
Asking the question, "can I fit inside you?"
Everyone told me to be with you only if I could give you
Everything I told you I couldn't give

You continue to complain of cold houses

These are all lies
Like the color of his eyes
Like the lines of a Whitney Houston interview with Diane Sawyer
white women have told me I can't have pleasure

And I plunged deeper and deeper into train lines
Where crust punks and hobos go to die

It keeps me up at night
Thinking of all the times I should have slapped you
And I didn't

When will you accept blackness as the
Exterminating Angel

And that there is joy in burning shit
With abandon

Them girls can talk about how
they have an affinity for cars and
wine and the shallowness of their brown
divorced of class

"Watch this poet say all the things we shouldn't have to say"

So much for visibility
our ribs are touching
it's not exactly the entire cage just a rib

Spore matter — I like the way it leaves dust
on both dead and living things alike
I rub my fingers back and
forth until my tongue swells and mouth waters
this is me stealing a precious moment in the day

This poem can do both
it can pool guilt and fuck
it can be political too, if you want to talk about disruption
it just keeps re-spawning and
deepening the dampness of the wet, juicy spot in
                    the middle of
                            the middle of
                                    that middle in

that bed that is not your own
it only gets that way when I'm alone
day dreaming of marches and
imagining meeting you in the South, where it'd have been
more kinky to be doing how I do now in the North and who it with
but this time with the lights on
flood lights, I like the way my pupils spread
under them and I can feel myself opening up
knowing you will save me from arrest
knowing we've both done enough time in
study groups to know our basic shared principle: no fucking on the left

"Watch this poet bleed like no other poet out there"

It's true because you believed in the idea and how it curled into you
curled up, pent up, totally bound and bonded to the big greying institution called:

Why do you need the answer to this anyway, why does there need to be a line to finish
this thought?
the ways we can imagine how people die so far away from us
the ways we don't even have to imagine we see it on the vine
people doing it /on it /for the gram

PRIMITIVE ACCUMULATION

If it's hysterical, it's historical
Reading like a commercial that holds you along the trip to sleep

I didn't know there was an alternative to capital
And that I could press one
One on one with my body against cement
One on one with debt because it's the definite lover
The complete God, walks with me in sleep
One on one because what happened at the bar
In my pants on your mouth does not make it
To the meeting even if everyone can smell me on you
Sweet and full of darkness
Demons
I believe that proper words are teachers
And police officers that restrain little girls
And don't worry when their bodies don't make a sound when their
skulls hit the concrete
But again
        One on
        One

Imagine all of the stories slaves would have written
If they didn't die writing with their flesh
Instead their flesh was for a sadistic master
and our |Age of Enlightenment|

Tell me when it hurts, I'll keep going

MOST OF THE PEOPLE WE LOVED DIED WITHOUT GRAVES

We start to fail when we think we can no longer win
And everything is comfortable still where it is
And the skin is just fact
Not remembering how it got there
But only realizing when it breaks and cracks that it's truly romantic to be temporal

You'd rather be guilty than learn from your mistakes
Let them know I'm the only one that can tear your insides out, acutely bring you under
heat lamps only for growing purposes so that any inkling of doubt can be cast away

Gulls screech into the streets hoping to bring some life to them and maybe even disease
Because isn't that the closest we feel
Splitting the soul in fourths, so we can wander and never rest

The
      People
            Want
                  To
                        Know
Is everything as fucked as they say it is?
In the metal, write your name
I want it on my chest
Like all slick, wet things
That go to rest there

The whiskey is always there for me to sidle up to

ATLANTIC

I could reach into the back of my throat and pull a gold ring
Whether power is going east or west
Whether there is an absence of gravity
Hymns sung on shorelines of modernity
In record shops with class driven disco
The weakening of economy this historical timeline
Pulls a thread that brings colonial projects
To meet here on an the avenue that knows me best
Property like energy is neither created nor destroyed
Fire is fire is ash and they all burn the same

In forests where things come alive
I can't say, "I want to undo myself, like thread to wrap around you"?
I can't say,
"These were the material conditions
Of your breath on my
Breath and we chose to take and
Cling closer to what
Primitive accumulation afforded us best: bondage"

Muttering something about diasporas
Muttering something about the flimsiness of white supremacy
But not when it's attached to lust or condemnation

I've been playing tarot with books
Looking at titles to spell your name
Not the spoken name but the name in
The form of a question that I don't want to know
The answer to

Because I already know the question I want to ask
I wanted to touch just a little bit longer
And that is all we had to lose
We gave up willingly

And the admission that these will be the last words to spend on commodities
To grope
And ask permission for eating
My ledge has become altar to sleepless nights

Children push boundaries because their bodies are endless
Stretching and sagging into youth into dust

I could see the film growing on the computer screen

Feeling myself break just to surround you

Recognizing the shredding of my own flesh on the back of my legs and that the
marks are definitely Permanent and will stay with me until my flesh sloughs away
I wouldn't ask for it any other way

Mirrors shaking
Waiting to break over heads
Have you ever felt anything more hateful

Pluto in Scorpio
Wild vibration
Building of a tomb
Watching your body die
While you're inside of it

LOOKING FOR STRANGE

I impaled myself onto
the history of Thursday
a length known in meters
something where only aloe plants can
become trees
a place where children grow without gas
an expansive organic place
a place you can put your vote behind
if only it was real
or what
the fuck ever

You couldn't even bring me the sea
this siren blares for you
is it a tearful ode or does this intervention break bricks?

People can tell that I am waking
into a form that isn't exactly a
Monday or even half of a quaking sound
that stutters along, only wishing that this affair
could break a police line
if Only

Fortifying the mythology that people like me
don't win
are wicked.
being the only pure glowing object, pooling
onto the border of where belly becomes pelvis
pelvis becomes emergency contraceptive

contraceptive only as a formless want of desire
I could tell by the lines on your palm,
that you were a John in your five other lives
only in this one you promised me Muir beach
I believed it

No, I don't drive but I thought it'd be a good idea
for us to pull up beside my childhood ideas of desirability
or more accurately, disposability
 just so we can laugh and say "you got that one right. Hallelujah"
or as Soleil tops this one off with "whatever"
because I'm tired, but not toothless, sometimes
my jaw makes shapes like that and the sound comes
out like "fuck, I'm actually sad" or
"we can end this. I don't care anymore. I just want it to stop."
It's the accent my grandparents gave me

I've already decided on which gait I'll pursue
walking out of cars and
into fifteen-year-old sexual awakening in Polynesian countries
I've already made plans on what to do with looks of pain
and for the most part. I won't be there. I won't be available

All my friends' teeth decided to commune with mine
now there is this crookedness in my expression
no long monotone
but resonant in an octave fluent in infections
a hole-growing farm for women

that grew up in disease but did not die and
had their glands age before they ever could
There being no place to return because
this was the beginning
young and angry. Years of being well-fed
served me well up until this moment
talking your mother off the ledge
of a car door on a workday
will she return?
will my body stop bleeding after 15 days?
I'm on the mend, perpetuate light
tell me to live "through this"
because I am dying, I haven't cummed enough for this to be happening

Maybe if we scream loud enough in this moment
things can finally end
we can move on and get older
with our respective wounds and pets named in our honor
on the days we were born in red pickup
trucks outside of parties wishing us well
instead the protagonist settles for guilt

It's my favorite truth
objects aren't supposed to be seen

I've doomed your bedroom to my (redacted)

A friend telling me a written word is not his to claim but instead is owned by the spirits
holding tribunals for war pig leaders
do you love the spirit that is in your life?
both living and dead. walking around hunched over
forgotten because no one asked what it had to eat or drink that day

A white woman comes running to me,
telling me she's won
and I know that her lover can't be mine
because mine is a love of partisans
aching for earthy mounds
while hers is out in the open, so we can all praise him
it's a birthday, similar to virginal anniversaries
and I'm not invited to the holy occasion
it's all screen printed on and feeling alright

When I heard you speak
I knew I needed to see the city's walls crumble
sometimes that's just what nationalism does to the body
the family man

KADDISH

The world blew up in my mouth
I felt it shake in my hands
bleed open
dive in
or fall in/fall out
looking for shelter
never guaranteed in a proclamation
an exit
a recall
I get to hear the news as I wake up

                    It's all birthed under a hard water moon

Twisted blackish brownish maybe grayish limbs
can do much to tell fortunes unknown
Like broken chicken bones
they swing and lie
on nightclub floors

It's dark blood magic
darker than the Caribbean
this is the duty of santos
real fucking brujas
giving their bodies
stretching in places, sown up and castrated by the world

   UNsilked:
The great house of the family and nation
is the twisted cosmology of the plantation
you never got to know the length of your own body beyond
the manic limbo it possessed

so the dance floor took you home
still feeling and
still in love
getting/giving your life to the Cabaret voodoo
pulsing
into Yemaya
in the sea

When I hear others voices
it isn't of complete destruction but
of uneven confused mistake

All my friends are sleeping

Your body is a drone because when I touch it, it just hovers there

you get tired of some things and other things, you just let stand on their own

Everyone is learning how to die in this new way
except it isn't new
body as a fault line
body that was never a body
wrong time and place to be a body

Dromomania | Strange Labor
It's never without intention
when editors ask you to write about "nature" or what "comes natural"
when the face
of nature is a bourgeois 18th century concept

primitively accumulated
from the inside // out
not meant for you to ingest
and the fact that nature poems
are the class enemy
and cement cages by tainted water
fields to work are what you know
but they want to see bloodstained sharp
edges silver on their pages
but you're still bleeding
from the truth
in the cyclical nature of crisis

The "body" poem, like
the nature poem
is the enemy
because it was never alive
and it's meant to remain that way
it is a request to exist
a resignation
not taking power
that is deserved
The confessional
is the enemy
it is the stand-in for a boss
who owns you down
to excretions from
battered, bruised, castrated parts
it is a demand to submit your soul to a property owner

But such generalized demands
have been made
we can say there are bodies
without homes, food, rest
that is why transportation centers
are home
so that the body without a
home can finally rest
even in motion
capitalist sleepwalking tricks
bodies are going to do what they do
but it's the people that die
inside of them

Some people want others
to see them burn in public
because at least that's what
they deserve
in death
not redemption
to be told "you're not wrong"
is a burnt offering
a token
for walking around with a half-eaten life

As black arthropods fill up
glasses of water with their bodies
could their bodies become

a body
when a body is seen as something
of worth
to be insect
is disposability
down to the Latin root
to be cut into
severely
routinely
without question
Dali thought ants were symbolic death
maybe because

I have extremely low arches
and never been properly introduced to the death poem
I know it's poetry for some to die
for others
to watch
selfishly
It's what some have the privilege to call the anthropocene

Viscus is the value begotten from labor
interwoven through our bodies
and not bodies
bodies that failed to become bodies
bodies that weren't able to become poems
because they were too manic
the value was never mine to give

It wasn't the way
Mercedes Eng talked about
how her father pleaded
to be seen as
equitable to whiteness
equity
being property
but how she talked
about how someone died
in the bowels of the state
the prison
which doesn't happen
in the form of a bang or a whisper or a crunching sound
but instead in
the slippage of skin
into other inanimate material twinning
becoming a shape of horror and puss
in flowing Pocahontas hair

Only then
did I feel myself
being allowed to collapse
and become a part of
the background
the linoleum floor, the genealogy
of extraction of raw materials
Someone's dead already
or someone

already died
inside

Will all our data soon
be collected
so that the future police
of the world
know exactly how we like to be fucked
hard and soft
with spit
drool coming down our
teared up faces
surprised orgasms
full of hate and fear of future planning
because Saturn always likes to weigh heavy on consequence
organs are definitely a consequence
and of course
how we want to be killed
it doesn't matter if it happens
on a TV screen or a computer screen repeatedly over and over because
the body is an open minefield for all of us to trip into
blow up
and die
a slow death
or alone in the regret and indifference
of cement jail cell walls, that get so hot
you dream of winter
or

fleshy sea floors that tug the body further down into depths
where
you dream of fire
but there is none, because that gas leak is occurring on a different coast

My grip is lax
yet
I can still feel it twitch inside me
it's begging for me to squeeze in more places than one

ELECTRIC WIZARD

Commodity commodity
It's the black commodity
Corrosive commodity
Burns through tin and aluminum
In my hair commodity
Black commodity
Holding animality
White girls can understand, it's close enough to the dog commodity
It fits in your bag, made to be in your life
In the company of fetish

      In which panel do I get to be Fred Moten or
      Frantz Fanon, so that you can think my words are pretty too?

      I want myself against everything
      Stay there and be burned into the mind
      Into the mind

      So god
      So god, so good
      Got soggy on my way here
      But
      So god
      If your church isn't handing me a metro card
      Then why isn't god saving our souls from capital
      This truly is heaven on earth

Heavy energy
Heavy life
Death in
Mundane out

My lover comes bearing coins
And I always know what time it is

    Death and war all by my side
    A year with pulse
    A year of dead teenage girls
    In jails
    Black oil snakes
    So good, so god
    The end and un end
    Everyone is learning how to drink poison

    The darkness of the south
    The blindness of the north
    The grand delusion of it all

    A hung moon

    Time of all time has ended
    With what is a poor substitute of equity

Sometimes death isn't even enough to make good on past grievances

Sometimes suffering for god isn't summed up in embracing the graveyard

Time of timed boundaries has ended

It began on the edge of a fence in a great hall exclaiming to no one in particular

"Watch me light myself on fire and burn for you"

As I tell this story about stingy lovers

    Or how about we did embrace the tomb

    Or how about we did win by losing

    Or how about "yeah, man, I'll miss you when you leave this city"

    And how we can't pronounce the word "touch" or

    "I need you now. but no, don't come over, I'm exhausted"

    But of course we settle for private property as an alternative because

    false gods taught

    Us well

    Everything is a joke with time

    In time, around it, scalping up roots that were supposed be to

    buried in our stomachs

I'm traveling along time to make up for wages

Lost wages in negative time

The kind without growth

The kind without organs

Body time

This internal clock breaks for you

But others will call it the selling of labor power

Labor power meaning desperation at the term "electoral activism"

Perverted time, obtuse because

I want to fight and care for friends at this edge of time

Explosion of Saturn time

Looking for soul in a leather jacket

I chose not to sleep through time

This time

The suffering made things feel more possible

I'm going nowhere fast, all of our secrets about the world

Aired out at this exact moment together

Walking diagonally speaking to God

Hoping the night doesn't eat too much of me

In the absolving time of night

Falling upwards longitudinally through history where mosquitoes

Grow living in the crochet text-flesh of our friends

Praying that it flows into what could be the constellation of bonds

Strong enough

Lighting a fire in the woods, hoping something good will see it

Hoping it's good enough for them

Telling us through the fire to use the sword to our advantage

Built in the blood of travel of the fool's journey

Running wet under the moon

Teaching myself how to cauterize a wound that's decades old

Licking away at a curse that isn't even mine to hold

On left handed coasts we lie

About how our bodies learned how to say hello

How we wanted to be in the light

In the dark

How we whisper things better left unsaid

Because everyone is searching for life and meaning

Everyone is in crisis and we just fell into the trap

We just wanted to experience death without it being mortal

We wanted to fail and believe there was a hereafter

And that there is something beyond blood and cum

Something beyond being a vampire

Something beyond dead

Even beyond that because then

There isn't even infinity and if there is, math couldn't count it

We lit a fire and everyone saw

The world ended and we still chose to live in it

Hoping for no return

STOP TEXTING ME

Progressive still means prisons

While the rich steal the future as if it were magic

And is that what the implementation of time really is?

I can repeat the same words I've said in the past just so you know

I'm forreal

And I want the end, and an orgasm for my trouble

So what I said, was

"Someone died, and we kept laughing

Buildings burned

Not in our favor. And the nurse still wants to know who

Is going to pass the afterbirth of future"

Evangelical hyperbolism of the binary pushing on tissue

No man is ever worth a line of poetry

But I still wrote

High on my own delusions

Whilst others lived inside of them

There was nothing you could say

Or do in that moment except fall

Over your own words via encryption

If not for the rigor of his absence

I would've not

Been equating lack for passion

And higher mental faculties to help us tire through the day

And that's what men do

And there are no good men

You like the noise of me

How I sit in the lining of where

Fat meets connective tissue with skin

That's where I lie inside you

LOVE LIFE

This is how the world ends
swallowing inside of us carcinogens
you can only hear me when I say "fixed capital"
"object" or "that's right, this is the political line to end all lines"
a love life
totally lush
pulsing
total desolate
feeling all spasm and highs
how cruel, kind of
love Life

Something like an absence of feeling, I never had permission to love you
never had permission to love
anyone
you can't love me the way I deserve to be loved
never
so, it makes sense
a love life
only on the weekends when you can't see me in the light
a real love life. A real girl with cottage parts
malting

My insides decided to hangout
with us
in public
in the cold
rotting
like a hollowed out
ornament

People die in private ways
our relationship to property

I get to hear about black people dying while I'm in the woods
historically a place for black people to die
hunted by dogs, raped, lynched
A sketch of patrols
It's the cops you love

Like when have I ever loved
life
really loved life
a love life
a horror
(spoken in a Baltimore accent)
a real love life
pain and secretions
overloaded
once and for all
a love life

A door in the trees
coffee stain smells in my nostrils
under a dying wild earthy vibration
the howling of coyotes

I ruined the home of spirit with my fingers
its web got tangled
in the hair
on my hands

I was falling apart as the woods were falling with me
into the hole of the city and the city
told me
us
that it was shaking
another dead black man
a constricted flesh
taunting
some who would call a bare life
not bare as the night sky against epidermis
but bare as not being born
and being forced to live

How many people like me could only exist on the margins straddling the
darkness
the marshy, dewy feeling of freedom
maroon
matching blood
under sun

I dreamt
I
was a rebel
in the bushes
hiding with you
but I realized
love could
only
be useful
via my corpse

I'll be here as the
world lurches
and folds upon
its own flesh
and hills
and taut musk
reeking of history
the jaggedness of the tree line

Someone is calling on the other line
mountains disappearing with the
turns of roads
the base of the mountain
reminding us that all are welcome to reasonable attainability
but the top of the mountain is negative infinity something that isn't quite true and
meant for peasants to have fever dreams about bread, champagne and opiates
I know about your lies, Mt. Shasta

We can only hope that when the gates of hell open up that evil takes us
because utopia is only for those who can afford it

We can imagine Anglo names that have
no function
and that's fucked up

The fault of mesas
I'm not meant to live in the woods
but to cut through them
vengeance is justified

abolition is my chariot
when children mourn
Philando Castille
and say
"You have rainbows in your heart"
I want them to know
there's a dead cop at the end of that rainbow
and we gonna be alright
I read sunset hills as
"suspect hills"
Because my hate cannot hide in the
expansiveness of
the day
or literally light

"Hope you feel better"
but
time
is built
like Pelican Bay
built up like
a love life
so instead
I hope you can bleed
in something that
isn't nice
or too expensive
and that others can

see it run over all our
pretty
things
that
can only
hope to be beautiful
so that
it can be a proper
love life

Hydrangeas
remind me that all
wounds are forgiven

I ran my fingers hard
against the edge
I welcomed splitting
not yet a burn
not yet a cut
trying to
decide how
it wanted to be fucked up

We have lovers to
text
as we lay side by side
wondering
what they ate

forgetting our
own pleasure in
the sunshine
and rumbling
inside of us
are we seeking
water
food
or
hurt feelings
divorce is an earned tree ring
me
matching with
you

Other's ghosts
becoming an other's
second act of being
ghosted upon
there are at least three in the room
there's at least an
incubation
stage
a sketch of Trotsky's
scheduled decline
of capital
stage theory // attachment Theory
a musical
          The Love Life

BLACK MASS

On Twitter stating you are "in general anti-millennial"
which is code for anti-black/brown/power
because we all know white people are disappearing from imaginations
just ask the Balkans
they're still waiting on becoming white

Hearts desiring adversaries
looking for strange but
the sun no longer sets me free

How black was our sabbath
people, like our white exes,
do funny things like show up to
marches for black women when they actually hate black women

13th and peralta
I'm in love with someone there
pretending not to be in love with me
my presence isn't necessary anymore
because I wasn't loud enough
because there wasn't enough space
between the actual city and those who tried to claim the city

But in general, I don't fight for souls already claimed
are you inviting me into the flames
of hell or are you actually conjuring the flames?

Black untitled without a place to settle
to credit
who cares
it's product to collect

The first men
never could've been children of water and wine
actual blood
carried by a starry bull and whatever else tries to enter

I'm not tryna assimilate or congratulate you for loving Beyoncé
Booker T already wanted that, manifested it
we're reaping it still unfree
Only black bougie jawns can eat up
all of us can get rich or die trying
most of the time it's dying, we try a little but it's half ass consolations
Black mayors
Black millionaires
THE Black writer on the press known for being knowledgeable
on such issues because they told you over brunch
that an Ivy league or well invested or well-to-do ancestor
paid for which if
you must know
they had a good advisor

Check this out
when I'm off work
my body still working and a vulture licking capitalist wants its labor power
for cheap of course

because the boss gets to cum
I get an iota of that and
some stupid promissory note that may never deliver
It goes to my liver
end of story
I pretend to love it and the boss pretends his life is worth living

To those that find themselves in darkness
and want to still keep walking through it
it's pain
get used to it
it's just a uterus shedding its lining

I was told I could taste anything I liked
but to spit out whatever could nourish me
so I walked around emaciated and clouded with hunger

Everyone wants the world back again

Wearing something tight enough to hold together my falling parts
Insides leaking onto the outside
A greedy spirit
How racialized the history of strangulation is
Either by rope
Or smoke
The burning of the Bronx in the 70s
On a MOVE

STOP TEXTING ME

I open up open up open open up open up

Until the walls sweat my name

Haunting isn't enough

I want to merge, live inside, split into your cells

Until flesh itself is only thought of as contextual

HOLLOW DELTA

Freedom in capital can be measured in furloughs

Diagonally, the lovers have merged with The State
The scene has merged with The State
The scene, like the barricades
Cannot hold
Out against Saturn
But who will pay the price?

Suicide happens by proxy
We get a dose of it in our feeds
Keeping us enraptured, utterly broken-hearted
Lonely like god

We lose in school

We lose in the hospital
What is given was haldol
Because the voices
We hear are loud
And external
Telling us:
"Struggle is gradual. Don't you want to function?"
But my body is in pain now
With my heart slipping out my anus
Because my sphincter got too weak from
The stress of holding shit in

We lose in church
Because the preachers, pastors, clergy all are silent
When black women are murdered by black ex-police officers
And black on black crime becomes null
Because this about lost masculinity
There it is
A hum of
"And the church say: AMEN"

We lose in work

We lose in romance
When we don't have to die
As a result of the passion of our lovers
Because we can't submit,
So we are beaten
Because only the abuse of our corpse
Can be proved innocent and worthy of love

I can tell you how this story should end
Something like
The Middle Passage reciting on Tuesday under a blood moon
Whispering:

I know people who would've been happy to just taste the sun once
Really

But this should be the true ending
We should repeat and fuck to:

If Black Lives Matter, then that means the destruction of America.
The entirety. That vibrates deep down into the core of earth, to emerge and
destroy Europe and the imaginings of it.

I'm the angel knocking on yr door
To let disease in
The place that I fit in doesn't exist,
Until I destroy it.

JASMINE GIBSON is a Philly jawn based in Brooklyn. She spends her time thinking about sexy things like psychosis, desire, and freedom. She is the author of the chapbook *Drapetomania*.

ACKNOWLEDGMENTS

Thank you to Mommy, Taylor and Mom Mom for making me the woman I am, and inspiring me to be the woman I want to be. Thank you John, for the caressing edits, and the love you've shown my words and me. Thank you Madison, for being a beautiful fish and my best friend. Thank you Nightboat, and particularly Lindsey Boldt for wanting this little July baby. Some of these poems have previously been published in the following publications in different formats: Alignment, as a limited edition chapbook, *Folder Magazine*, *Fanzine*, *The Journal Petra*, *The Poetry Project Newsletter*, *The Felt*, *Queen Mob's Tea House* and in the chapbook *Drapetomania*.

NIGHTBOAT BOOKS

Nightboat Books, a nonprofit organization, seeks to develop audiences for writers whose work resists convention and transcends boundaries. We publish books rich with poignancy, intelligence, and risk. Please visit our website, www.nightboat.org, to learn about our titles and how you can support our future publications.

The following individuals have supported the publication of this book. We thank them for their generosity and commitment to the mission of Nightboat Books:

Elizabeth Motika
Benjamin Taylor

In addition, this book has been made possible, in part, by a grant from the New York State Council on the Arts Literature Program.